PAINTING THUNDER

PAINTING THUNDER

POEMS BY ROBERT JUDGE WOERHEIDE

ROBERT B. WOERHEIDE

iUniverse

PAINTING THUNDER
POEMS BY ROBERT JUDGE WOERHEIDE

Copyright © 2024 Robert B. Woerheide.

All rights reserved. No part of this book may be used or reproduced by any means, graphic, electronic, or mechanical, including photocopying, recording, taping or by any information storage retrieval system without the written permission of the author except in the case of brief quotations embodied in critical articles and reviews.

iUniverse books may be ordered through booksellers or by contacting:

iUniverse
1663 Liberty Drive
Bloomington, IN 47403
www.iuniverse.com
844-349-9409

Because of the dynamic nature of the Internet, any web addresses or links contained in this book may have changed since publication and may no longer be valid. The views expressed in this work are solely those of the author and do not necessarily reflect the views of the publisher, and the publisher hereby disclaims any responsibility for them.

Any people depicted in stock imagery provided by Getty Images are models, and such images are being used for illustrative purposes only. Certain stock imagery © Getty Images.

ISBN: 978-1-6632-6486-2 (sc)
ISBN: 978-1-6632-6485-5 (e)

Print information available on the last page.

iUniverse rev. date: 07/23/2024

Dedicated

To my father,
for everything.

This poor forsaken man, who, if any mortal could,
might have been pardoned for regarding
himself as thrown aside, forgotten and left to be the sport of
some fiend, whose playfulness was an ecstasy of mischief.

Nathaniel Hawthorne, *House of Seven Gables*

Contents

Introduction xi

A Note 1
Collapse 3
Mother 4
Paint Thunder 7
Scratching Poems 11
Demolition 12
Corona 13
Four Lines 14
Little Storm 15
Ideal Reader 16
Fibonacci in Thirds 17
Revolt 18
Future String 22
Sun and Darkness 23
Doors and Bolts 25
Backpack 26
Brush Strokes 29
Redwood Seed 31
I Remember 32
Draft 2 35
Little Man John 36
A Message to my Son 38
Graveyard 40
Nightfall 41
Penis Envy 43
Puberty 44
Crafting Hours 47
A Note 49
Familiar Storm 51
Eliot's Epitaph 53
Call 54
Disease 55
February 57

Growth in Winter	59
Poem for a Wart	60
#Metoo Manhood	61
Clock	63
Seven and Eight and Nine	64
White Cat	65
Locus Angst	67
Red Shift	68
Grow Legs and Walk	70
The Eternal Space	72
re-member childhood	75
Absence	77
Black Dog	79
Note to Myself	82
Muse	83
Circle Perspective	85
The Bird Feeder Outside My Window	87
Poet	89
Dark Figures	90
Rain Clock Poetry	92
Bong Hit	94
Movement	96
Barefoot Long Game	99
Born Into Rain	100
You are Here	102
Oxygen Deprived in a Cave with Plato	103
Padding Around my Apartment Thinking on a King's Roux	105

Introduction

This poetry collection was written over the course of sixteen months—from January 2020 to April of 2021—and is intended as a companion to my previous collection: *Providence in the Fall of a Sparrow*. Although readers will benefit from understanding the thematic connection between this collection and its predecessor, I've designed either collection to stand on its own.

In "Poem Sixty" of *Providence*—the final poem of that collection—I called on the listener to "paint thunder." It was a metaphor I couldn't shake off and I've used it as the seminal metaphor in the creation of this collection. As such, I've shifted (but not abandoned) the elements of birds to focus on the active engagement of painting thunder using words.

As my readers will know, my life has been a stormy one, so it is not a difficult task for me to paint thunder. Whether I've done it well is for you to determine.

In these poems I have pushed myself to create works which are more intricate and nuanced. For that reason, some of them may at first seem less immediately accessible. Please make no mistake: my reader is always my priority. None of these were written with vanity or self-importance. Good writing always puts the reader first.

What I've done here is challenged myself to write more complex poetry, and therefore I'm sometimes asking my reader to take a little more time to understand the layers of a poem. Some of these contain poems within poems (if you pay attention to the vertical first-letter structures of the stanzas, for example). Others are simply more abstract than I typically write. Most, however, use the straight-forward voice with which I am most comfortable. I leave it to you to uncover which is which and determine whether I should quit my day job.

My favorite poets are Robert Frost and Billy Collins, so I am always desirous of accessible poetry. I hope you find these to be accessible and heartfelt, and that a line here or there reflects upon some of the joy or pain you might feel in your own life.

I would like to thank my support system for their indefatigable love: Bob, Jenny and Phil, Amy and Bo, Kate and Pat, Amy S, Stefan, each of my nieces and nephews, and my friend Fred. I would like to also acknowledge that I would not have been able to craft this collection without the no-nonsense tutelage of my mother, Marie Judge, a fine writer herself who passed away during its creation. Over a lifetime she taught me the two best things a writer can learn: Written language is miraculous; all good writing is hard won.

As usual you were correct, Mom.

A Note

From your uncle or your father or your brother,
it doesn't matter which—
in the end, it all comes from the same place.

Life is a strange bereavement of battles.
Arrows and slings from every angle.
While victories lift us aloft

alongside quiet and deeply felt defeats
we are convinced no one else can see.
Let me just say, in case it is helpful,

there isn't anyone here who doesn't understand
in personal ways—
at which you can only guess while we can only guess yours.

But I knew you when you were a child.
And I still see the same heart,
the same spirit alive amidst the hammering

of life. It is not a depressing thing
except that we might think it so.
It is a shared communion of suffering.

It is better than death, surely,
and better than thinking we are alone in pain.
It is your childlike spirit resisting the wearing-away.

It is your big heart,
your compassion, your soul.
Whispering against the fear.

It is all of the cosmic vibrations aligning you and me
and these words while I write them.
Maybe not whispering at all.

Maybe just saying it like it is:
Don't give up;
Embrace the blue and send it away.

Look it straight in the eye and remind it
we are the same purity who first opened our eyes
to this wild spectrum.

Give it a hug, and wave it
friendly,
out the door.

Collapse

Coffee cups and crayons
wrist bands
bedsheet ghosts
one beautiful nurse
and visiting hours
no belts or buckles
or shoelaces—strings
for jugular constriction
discharge a delicate dance:
not too much push
not too much pull
schedules on white boards
group and group and meals
served through a square
in the wall
personal items secured
scrubs and medication
stories paused or abandoned,
or not yet begun, or
newly started—
like a novel, left on a table

Mother

Does it hurt, mom,
the pain?
As we worry about you,

is your death bed soft?
Are we comforting your body and spirit?
Have we remembered everything?

Is it close, mom?
Do you see the veil?
Have the things you've wanted come to be?

Is the exchange you made with us,
giving birth and raising the four of us,
is it a fair one?

I look at your drawn face, tired eyes,
mouth open, hours away from death
and feel far away from you.

As you would likely feel too:
I can hear you,
"I look like death."

Can you feel me still?
Are you and I lost in darkness?
Do you remember? Is there remembrance?

Do the birds continue to sing for you, mom?
Does the memory of two metro-station violins still resound?
Bach upon the tiles and in the noon spring air.

Do you hear every precious memory
of your entire life
before I was even born?

Do you remember all the little joys
and the hardships,
and the first moments of every feeling?

Are these memories for me to carry?
How can I lift the spirit
of your life when I am only a son?
Maybe you just tell me
to put together photographs of you,
throughout your lifetime,

and marvel at the distance
of this mercurial existence,
so much found poetry.

Words and music and prayers,
and advice sometimes spoken or implied,
and frustrations and inevitable miscommunications.

And simple things.
Like a cat.
Or brown sugar.

Or the chime of a clock.
All this beautiful chaos
is life, and life is also death.

Shall I stop the pendulum
upon your corporal parting, while still
winding the springs for another hour?

Mother.
Who taught me.

Mother.
Who gave me scars and kisses.

Mother.
Who lives within.

Mother.
I am now without.

Mother.
Who has already answered.

Paint Thunder

Rattlesnakes and a flashlight,
around desert rocks, just after
late afternoon has given in to gloaming.
This is the end of his thousands mile trip,
going west first and east second—
the latter with his children in tow.

The innumerable hills are crested in dust, as everything
in this unusual suspense of Texas is.
There are an improbable number of
dirty SUVs and trucks smattering the road,
driving hilltops and navigating overflow bridges
among the flooded river passes.

He's driven dozens of miles, by now, along
these unscrupulous pathways, several raging
flooded overpasses, signs with warnings,
and the mounting thankfulness that this late and tired
camp for his family, will bring them rest and companionship:
a simple reverie at the end of a journey's day.

But when he reaches their encampment,
settles on a place to pitch and fire and cook,
the dark is nearly there, and the wind
is angry with unstated complaints, it seems—all fury
and no sound except the ghost wail and slap of gusts.
And the dust permeates everything.

The fireworks begin to glint and thunder in the distance
from the yokels with their vehicles pumped on Viagra—
a shout against the beauty of the sky, and
the landscape of which their diesels know nothing.
And the dust becomes everywhere with the wind.
And the wind becomes everywhere with the dust.

So he scurries to make camp
before the storm overrides the chance.
The dust and wind are harbingers,
metaphors he should know better.
But in those moments just before,
when he is walking his daughter to see nature,

when he is teaching her the beauty in a rattlesnake,
there is a moment when he is just a father
aware of his daughter's remarkable spirit,
and how she trusts him to keep her
safe.
Even if there are rattlesnakes.

The thunder of fireworks paints the sky.
The red dust permeates everything.
It's a parasite infecting eyes and skin
and coating every surface like
fast-working algae multiplying
with supernatural determination.

And damn if the tent won't post.
And damn if the rod doesn't break.
And damn if the dust isn't willing to ebb.

So they drive back along the same shit-dust roads
and flooded overpasses and warning signs, driving by
the same yokels and their oblivious F150s.
Blackness descends its canvas,
and Texas provides no apology for
the noise or the smoke or for anything.

And as if consumed by the state, tired and frustrated,
they enter Walmart and buy the first Coleman tent
they can find, and drive back again along the same roads
and floods and trees stunted dark now,
from which he must draw patience
in the blackness, pushing dust,

when they and it and everyone
painting thunder should sleep.
The wind is a physical force.
This is the time for a cave,
in a place that wants to kill monkeys without shelter.
There is no forgiveness for lacking resources.

Better to let things dry and rust,
give in to the dust of fury wind,
after a journey that loops back on itself perpetually.
Instead he posts the flimsy tent,
marking the spot and planting the pins in the ground.
The hand of the wind slaps from each side

against the face of shelter
against the idea of peace or happiness.
It strikes its blows down upon them
bending the ceiling and whipping the walls
and laughing the goddamn dust into their lungs.
While the sky memorizes strontium carbonate and calcium chloride,

just for a moment before it forgets into fading
double after-image,
and he finds small victory in the stability
of shelter, as if a rattlesnake beneath rocks.
Pause.
There is always beauty in the nature of things.

Like the simple gratitude of his children
when he opens the tent,
finds them awake and nervous, but managing
this unfamiliar situation quietly against
the anger of the wind, tent bend-lean, and he asks,

"Do you guys want to go to a hotel?"

•

In my dream again, my daughter asks,
"What does it mean, daddy?"
and my son, forever two-years old
asks me the same with his round blue eyes
as I answer,
"Thunder is the sound you hear before the storm arrives."

Scratching Poems

Worn down to a stub
near the padded room,
which is blue not white
like you always see in the movies.

Yells from a nearby hallway
elicit urgent orderlies,
buttons pushed for large, black,
red-shirted security.

The screams sound male,
but it's a female, one
nurse tells another. A female
willing down the walls with her deep voice.

The kind woman with the
hamster face, perhaps? Losing
her electro-shock virginity.
Last night she was reading, and laughing

with eyes that always smiled.
Even as we all sat, worn down,
like a tiny golf pencil,
scratching poems until discharge.

Demolition

There is a hole in the ground I'm watching.
I knew the house that used to stand there.
Now it is erased—a sign on the front yard says, "Demolition."
And there is caution tape everywhere.
There were Christmases ago when those neighbors would arrive
with cheer, but that is long gone.
Just as their house is now.
Vacant. Torn from tip to toe.
I have little more idea where they are than they do where I am.
But I've watched their house come down.
Have they?
There are questions the past always brings into the present.
They bought it in the 1980s, and there used to be a child held in
the back.
A kind of mongrel, the rumors said.
He probably only had personhood disability.
I was told through neighborhood chatter he lived in a closet.
Where later was built a bathroom.
And now the whole place is gone.
Demolition put a giant hole in the ground
with a pile of dirt measuring all the cubic yards needed
to fill in a new story.
It had no chance, such a small house.
It was lucky to survive as long as it did
among the bigger houses.
Now it will be forgotten,
like the child,
like the neighbors,
like the years I spent next door.
Forgotten to everyone as if it was only a giant gap.
Something to be demolished or filled anew.
As if it never existed.

And a new house will be put in its stead.

Corona

My wife says
I don't have coronavirus,
even though there are centipedes in
the dryer machine

and everything smells
different.
Of course one has
nothing to do with the other.

This whole mess
was brought to you
by the united
states of Chinese America

and the glorious
inability to read,
thanking god with a lower
g almighty

that we still have
some kind of ability
to speak
or write,

while some of our shoulders
hurt
and some of
us can think.

Four Lines

Four lines
in A-A B-B

is all it took to set the hook
for this boy and poetry

Little Storm

There are clouds alongside sunlight.
A rumble of distant thunder.
And I am excited to welcome you.
Bring the ozone.
Little storm.

In my imagination you rain down.
And broil and toss.
A thunder tumble.
Trees dance dance dance.
Little storm.

I am not working.
You are welcome to come.
I hear you.
I am of the same spirit.
Little storm.

Do you need words of encouragement?
Are you moving to other parts?
Whom are you washing today?
They must need it more in that direction.
Little storm.

Pass along but know I saw you.
I wave my spirit in your direction.
I will see you again in friendship.
I will listen to the water-wind when you choose to wash me.
Little storm.

Ideal Reader

My ideal reader has died.
It's terrible news, I know,
especially since I watched her go into the ground.

The last thing we spoke of was how
easily I might be able to buy a house.
Which did not at all measure up to

her voice in my head, telling me this sentence
could be better,
or this story is good.

What am I to do now that she is gone?
I never invited her to become
the person through whom I passed all the letters in my head.

I'm not sure when it started,
but that's really not the point.
It seems I'll have to find another ideal reader.

Can one do that, like changing tires?
How do I shift the voice in my head, after so many years?
Do I have to?

Fibonacci in Thirds

    The word for

'Father' was some version of 'pather'
in the beginning, linguists surmise,
before the Helenic, Italic, Arabic, Germanic tree branched out
our words, evolving through throats and tongues.
now we scratch down the
argument of which came first, with our fancy thumbs and larynx,
connecting thought to understanding,
connecting self to other,
identifying the first need for color and lines.

For our species, perpetual categorization is
instinct—like seeking food and shelter to sustain against this
battering existence.
our feelings, categorized; thoughts, categorized; words,
naturally: categorized.
and the run-on sentence of our history
capitulates to no one. A proto, paleo, prehistoric
conglomeration of self
interest.

Forgetting what we know about
intentions or regret, there is something
beautiful in the shambling, ill-constructed architecture
of our complexity—how we've shaped our
nature in our own image.
a foolish endeavor, but one taken on with bravado at least,
concocted with the arrogance of every firing neuron
circling electricity in our skull.
in the end it will be written, they were

    for the word.

Revolt

The president sends federal
officers to kidnap
citizens.

Something seems wrong.

I was born in 1977
clutching a 1789 constitution,
always believing

these guys got something right.

I sat stairsteps, thinking
about how this special cloak
could not be trampled upon.

We the people.

Representatives and taxes and
liberty.
The best of us, right?

In order to form a more perfect union.

But since then, as a boy,
childlike, I've see it wash away.
I've watched your presidents

Bush and Clinton and Bush again.

Sitting, listening to your television.
I'm saying there is something
wrong here

in our interpretation.

Maybe you're lazy
or maybe I'm crazy
I've already been told.

And so might they.

Simple.
Mark the lines.
Use words to delineate the rules.

Age twenty five years.

Maybe we already know the deck is
stacked,
chosen by the legislature thereof.

Probably we think ourselves better.

These men wrote
words that were intended,
no person shall,

trample upon

by our misunderstandings
of perspective.
Forgetting simplicity.

There's Ben

loading a gun to blow
into the face of Donald Trump,
in the middle of 5th Avenue.

There's Jackson jackass

telling me to write
words that will irritate.
Cause he didn't really mind

irritation.

Sole power to Jefferson
with his pink bedroom
and ephemeral negro lover.

About which we won't speak.

You can smell the antique
bedrolls and wood.
Alongside the sunshot

in the room where he died.

Imperfection among
simplicity.
As with less verses fewer.

It's a simple thing of grammar.

We forgot.
There is no fake news except
whatever you believe.

You see

we are all wrong.
Especially you
and especially me

especially them.

Twist the Covid frame
and tell yourself
it's all the same.

Or that's your favorite

dish.
But in the end
you and I should know better:

that this isn't right.

Something is wrong
here in the land of
brave and free.

As we grab

our bank account
and sleep with it.
How many dollars

does it take to forget

what we should have known
all along?
There is something wrong.

Future String

The thing with which poets and philosophers always struggle
is the future, as if we don't understand
it's in front of us.

The past is not the best predictor of the future,
nor is the present;
which is why

we can't wrap our heads around the prism of time.
Neural elasticity can't develop enough,
or prune neurons

around the concept that we can't understand the irreverent
string-theory of possibilities—
banging our heads

against unknown avenues of thought.
So we try our best to map out the mess,
write words and draw lines.

As if anything was under our control
to begin with.

Sun and Darkness

I am here, mom, squatting in the shade
during my work break,
thinking of you.

Dead now four months
to the day.
And me, still working the same

similar job one hundred percent.
Two dumpsters and the restaurant
back door, have no idea

how two conflicting concepts can exist
at the same time:
How we could be so comfortable with death

and yet be lost to it.
Find it hard to fathom.
Find it hard to see each other within

the dark perpetual
closed space with no music
and no movement.

I am still exhausted and alive
sometimes avoiding the sun,
and you dark deep, without it.

I would like to telephone you.
It would make a good conversation
and we would laugh

about the absurdity and wonder
over death and life.
It would be very Edgar Allen Poe, our phone call.

And I would ask, "Are you cold?
Is your body at peace?"
You might say, "Yes, a little. And yes.

But it's not so bad
in this peace-dark,
with memories forgotten.

And there are no bills,
no phone calls,
no worries or appointments to measure time."

I think of your corporal self decaying and feel tears.
And I realize there is one thing I forgot to say:
I will miss you.

Can I tell you that over our Poe connection?
This imaginary landline
reaching through sun and sweat and

earth?
Darkness?
Silence?

Where does the measure meet
between love and time,
or timelessness?

Doors and Bolts

Let's start from the beginning of all the questions
you want to ask,
but don't want to trespass upon.

Before I say what I want to say.

Let's begin with the simplest.

There was an insect, crawling along the floor,
while he told me the presumptions of all
who know more,

while knowing less.

And I was happy for his ignorant freedom.

We both were caged within impenetrable steel and plexiglass,
behind locks, with book in hand, ignoring insults, wise
to the fact that they knew not

the lay of the land.

Or hadn't seen friends return with new knowledge disturbing them.

We'd read it all before they had even written words on the pages
of their faces,
this insect and I,
crawling on our tiny legs to get nowhere.

And we were happy for our caged freedom.

He and I, and I and he, looking at each other.

While we circled, seeking an escape
which would never present itself
against the doors and bolts.

Backpack

Can I write this pain down?
Can I capture it and print it with words and ink?

If so, please let me know, because this backpack is heavy.

My therapists tell me, in other words and specifically,
I have room in my backpack.

But damn if this walk to class isn't heavy.

I reach into this metaphor, and open my notebook.
There are marks from everyone who has written on me.

Can I find something from the two who weigh upon me?

Sue is there to tell me confidence and talent.
There is the poet in biology who sat beside me and loved animals.

Fred always with exactly the right perspective push.

My father, who teaches heroism.
Steve, who teaches poetry accessible and unforgiving of political bullshit.

Brittney, who redefines me every day.

Box, so frustrated after he keeps losing chess against me,
but thankful for another match.

Let me turn the page to see

if there are any other memos touched upon my life.
The pages are full of ink.

Jenny, patient and growing and saying

"I can fly out there today if you need me."
Phil telling me not to click the fork against my teeth.

There's a note about waiting in line for Floyd tickets

while throwing a football in the parking lot
with strangers at 5:00 am.

In the margin there is something about
poetry, and imagining
there must be one single word that encapsulates every truth.

Here are the essays I wrote into the night

and received teacher's positive feedback.
Here are the stories I scratched, little miscarried embryos.

There are pens and pencils in here too.

King and Ondaatje and Shakespeare and Poe.
Dylan and Yorke and Waters and Reznor.

What a variety of colors in this pocket of my backpack.

Where can I find the paper or implement
to put down this pain?

Then at the bottom, crimped under several books

about evolution and political and
literary theory,

I find something I write myself

sometime in the future,
when I am done with class:

"There is no eraser;

A whole lifetime will result in lines of writing.
Before and after you have taken down all the photos

of your unrequited love

and agreed to move on.
Simply write:

'Carly on your sheep,
and Dylan with your smile,

please forgive me.'

Then put your backpack on again
and walk forward."

Brush Strokes

Let me paint this picture
and maybe you'll understand.
There is a complication between
the fragility of truth and the strength of conviction.

I am trying to mix this pallet
of human experience color.
It isn't easy;
the mixing or the experience.

Let's look through a box of photos,
or peek through a door,
or braid each other's hair,
shall we?

Let's talk secrets,
about how we don't like
what we see
or feel about feelings.

Let's grow perspective,
because seasons pass within a yawn
of our strong bark.
Together we will love the storm.

It won't be easy but we'll
mix this pallet.
We'll paint the story,
ever evolving, this

love and pain,
and persistence,
and leaves growing
along branches.

Suckers, they'll call us
drawing water from
the roots
seeking the light

below taller branches.
Determined they'll say
to each other, green
with small leaves,

simple things they try
to sucker upon
like water,
but don't understand.

It will be a story
that others will read
and recognize.
Take the brush

and dip the paint
to run across canvas.
Draw brush across cotton
fields waiting to receive.

See what colors
you decide.
See what colors
we will paint together.

Redwood Seed

Planted by your ancient mother while she dreamed of birth,
before this writer or reader, or any of our parents,
were born. Before we had thought to grow.
When things were quiet, before the noise.

You grew silently. Before swing sets
or divorces or marriages. Prior to
degrees and parenting tricks. Anticipating
the instant-blip of pagers and social media.

Before all that, and long before.
Even since the start of what we could understand,
you've stood there. While
we've tried to scratch our feelings into words.

There's ancestory in your age,
that we simple monkeys can't understand:
The smell of your bark mixing with
the morning air when everything is quiet without watching.

Standing still, growing slowly, seemingly forever.
While we shrink against the weather, bruised and guessing
for the next precipice. Trying
to figure the gravity you've already long understood.

Will you tell me, underneath your leaves admiring,
is this some high-flight delusion?
Bark, along my fingers. Feeling the years between us.
There is light filtered unfiltered, somewhere, I suspect.

And over this modest composition you grow, slowly,
from that first seed of wisdom,
given to you by your mother, which diagramed:
seek the light.

I Remember

My love, I remember
all those times you don't.

Like when you asked me what I was listening to
and I responded Nine Inch Nails, Mozart, and Pink Floyd

and you said, "That's cool. I like listening to different music too."
And I was happy you understood.

Or that time you wanted to take me to a club.
As if together, we would ever do that:

Move among music and sexual bodies.
Free to be ourselves.

I remember when you walked up to me and said
the detectives had cornered you,

and I asked why and you said, "You!"
It is alongside my memories

of you about to jump into your death or
at the least two broken legs and maybe your back,

and I pulled you into my apartment to cunnilingus
as an apology for the universe hurting you so much.

I remember you sobbing through the floor
until the neighbors could hear how much you missed me

as I drove away to another state,
when I didn't really want to.

These things I remember.
Like when you argued with me about being a side bae

to a girl we both found attractive.
Saying it was silly, when it wasn't.

I remember driving overnight and sleeping
for thirty minutes in a rest stop.

I remember arriving with flowers at dawn,
but not before I bought a toothbrush to wash my breath.

I remember playing our song on my cell phone
as I walked into the door

and fearing I'd find you with her
but grateful I didn't.

I remember thinking I hope you know
you can always come to me

and sleep under my porch if you're
homeless and we aren't allowed to be together

because my probation officer
has threatened me with prison.

I remember you short-haired
and crying a little when we met again

on main street in St. Charles
when you were getting assaulted by that man

whom I thanked for being your friend,
without knowing I would prefer to fight him.

And then finding it out, stuffing that feeling down
so it could haunt me forever.

I remember driving with you
through the sunlight

top-off Corvette with Metric playing loud.
I remember you as my student

telling me you had stories I'd inspired.
I remember standing in the middle of the gymnasium

while coordinating the senior presentations,
and hearing you say I was the person you chose

to thank for inspiration.
I remember saying yes and no and yes

I remember betrayals and frustrations.
I remember people telling me to run from you.

I remember dates I had with you when it was actually Seth,
or Melinda.

I remember sex with B—
spitting in my mouth and whipping me.

I remember learning you in more names
than you realize were even there:

People inside our orbit I had to map
and memories I still hold.

I remember being an observer to all of this and more
and not having anyone to understand

the totality of what it is I've seen,
and remember.

Draft 2

Here is draft 2
not anywhere
while being everywhere
you might presume

Here is draft 2
in a drawer
waiting
listening

Here is draft 2
along the street
in a gutter watching
trees bend with rain

I am draft 2
but don't tell
our secret
to anyone

I have patience
they would
not understand
and secrets

That are worth
a third draft
within dark cedar
smelling sweet

And mothballs
and blankets
waiting always
in the dark for you

Little Man John

The little, fat man, garbed in
construction-vest yellow,
shuffling off in confusion and hatred,

turns—no, rotates his half—
and extends his short middle finger,
vitriol consuming his stooped face.

You motherfucker
he hisses, but not loud enough
to get caught by the others—

the suits around him.
Who undoubtedly hear
regardless.

This little man is fuming
with disgust
over just about nothing.

Self-important is he.
And all the insignificant
slights of his life

are always locus external.
What makes me laugh
is not how pathetic he looks,

instead,
I find humor in the fact
that he has consumed

himself with anger at me.
When all of it, the irony,
is only hurting himself.

It would be easy to say,
fuck you too, little, frustrated man,
but instead I will leave him

to do that on his own.
It's like watching a top spin,
and marveling at the rotation.

He wants nothing more in this world,
— not peace or love or productivity—
than to see me in pain.

How sad, this little man.
How unfortunately sad.
To be so narrow and blind.

So I will just smile and shake my head,
and wish him the best.
Off you go, little fellow.

I'm sorry your life
is so tough,
and your mind is consumed

by little hatreds grown
big, branching out all the sunlight
from your snow-globe sky.

A Message to my Son

There are people who will tell you things,
like how to be or who you are,
or how your fathers were.

There are half-truths,
and ghost stories,
neither you nor I will understand.

Certainly, they won't,
these people,
with their convictions of how to be.

There are no words other than platitudes
for photographs that capture souls
and moments long ago.

Imagine that moment,
in Ireland or Germany,
before our lineage traveled.

We can see it in their still faces
and read their names on stone,
captured black and white.

But life is always
in full color.
Just as theirs was,

and ours has been and will be.
We capture and are captured.
Single moments or truths

along a string of reality
which cannot be contained
or explained within or without

all the complexity of their
stumbling lines of
dot-to-dot certainty know-better.

I could say to you,
I've never been understood,
and I would

except that might give you pause
in your own struggle to be
understood.

I can only guess
our fathers felt the same frustration
alongside the same peace.

They lived and died,
as you and I will.
They were perfectly imperfect.

And there are many things worse
than that human fate,
and not much better realistically achieved.

Don't doubt yourself.
The wind is full of noise,
but that isn't a mark against its nature.

Nor are we marked against ours.

Graveyard

There we are, the two of us, poking around gravestones.
Looking at names and figures on granite.
It's the start of a New England winter,
but you and I have given things a drive.

I'm too young to know how the final bell rings,
and you're close to my age now; neither of us
has any reason to understand.
We will both change before we are put underground.

But the granite never changes.
Erosion is only surface; there are bodies underneath.
People born in 1698 or 1924. Names. Children.
These facts cannot be altered.

And why mother and son visit this place,
imparting sacred feelings,
is no more a question than an answer,
as the rest of the world trembles on.

Nightfall

The haunted trees outside my window as a child
were visible to me even though
I was trapped in my bed by circling wolves,
demanding me to sleep.

I couldn't move or they'd attack.
They were my counting sheep.

So I would look to my left,
without of course moving my body
lest the wolves became aware
I was cheating,

and I'd watch their black limbs
silhouette quiver in the wind.

They never frightened me.
I was comforted by their movement.
They were not afraid to be awake in the dark,
or to move with the elements of nature.

Sometimes, as I understood then and still do,
they are willing to take a lightning strike

just so we don't.
They aren't concerned with wolves,
or marriages or politics—
not that either of the latter are much different.

But they did seem concerned with
boys trying to sleep and offering them peace.

Those trees have grown with me,
as I assume they still stand.
Perhaps one day I will return to them
and thank them for teaching me

any storm can be weathered.
Especially when there are wolves circling.

Penis Envy

My wife is sleeping, and my child is within her.
Both of these things fascinate me—
not that she is asleep, of course,
but that she is here with child.

There is something which has constantly
befuddled men. I read volumes on it when
slogging through studies of literary criticism.
Us guys will never understand

what it's like to grow a life inside of us.

It's assumed this is the reason we
start wars or write books or
do everything men do
while not growing children inside ourselves.

So the tendency is not to give too much credit
to the other sex, lest we lose what little power we have.
None of which is meant to say we aren't valuable;
just that we're self-conscious,

the way boys are when they don't know the answer.

Puberty

If you don't like confessions or sex,
better to skip this one.

Which I presume means
no one will skip it.

Fair warning. Which is more than most
of us get in the age of 2021.

As when I learned
something alternately intimate

from my wife
before I left for a work shift—

as if that was the time to tell me—
and who later told me she feared I'd be angry.

Perhaps it will help
my dreams haunt less

if I put this into writing
instead of every night trying

to find her among an orgy
of permutations she laid upon me.

You've never figured out
you are sexually stuck in your twelfth year.

You talk shadow work;
for me that was never my shadow.

It was bright in the sunlight
as part of the story of me, left

along the road
a marker of my youth and journey.

I've never shied away from it.
Back when I grew up, there was no need

to pretend things
were or were not.
We didn't have to pick genders
or decide how we should love.

For that matter,
we needn't worry about whom we looked upon.

So in case it's helpful
to someone reading these words:

Those times he touched me and I touched him,
or she touched you and you touched her,

were just part of growing up.
And ancestors in caves did that too, during puberty.

Am I old enough to say
I grew up in a different era?

I mean nothing written here to be offensive
lest cable news or social justice

warriors rain down hell upon
my earth,

like white drops upon skin,
while afterward

we both listen to Floyd's "Have a Cigar,"
and listening to the lyrics he says,

"It already is a monster."
And I glow inside, knowing the intimacy

of what he means,
at twelve years old.

These are the movements of puberty
the movements of growing into

our adult selves
who love our wives and husbands.

Being whoever they might.

Crafting Hours

There is a time
when I get home late at night and the darkness folds
over us like a blanket,

when I write.

Sometimes I know what I'll say;
other times I don't.
Either way it's always a joy to develop words

in the secret of darkness.

I might talk about my children or my wife.
I might explore a brief inspiration drawn to life.
Maybe these dark, quiet hours of craft will bring

a new understanding.

Mostly though, I try to frustrate my way
through an idea
about how I can better express

all the inexpressible understandings I have gained.

Which is when I lean on my tutors—
the people who have taught me—
noted poets and un-noted ones as well,

like the homeless man,

who had a pretty good poetic voice
speaking in my memory.
I met him on a street in San Diego.

Or my professors and their books.

Everything seems to coalesce in these hours—
spilled blood drawn into the middle
of some surface-tension grasp.

I want to place my finger on it and draw

the color upon the surface.
There must be a place for these feelings.
There must be words for my thoughts.

Painting thunder can't be so hard.

Certainly I can figure a way to express
how everything has turned out in different ways than expected.
There are apologies tangled with pains of

irrefutable injustices.

There are also glorious insights I want to share.
All of which are somehow
contained in the tapping key strokes

of these moments,

while the fan hums sleep-tones,
and the outside world has for a while let me go
so that I might be myself

trying to tell you who we are.

A Note

From your uncle or your father or your brother,
it doesn't matter which—
in the end, it all comes from the same place.

Life is a strange bereavement of battles.
Arrows and slings from every angle.
While victories lift us aloft

alongside quiet and deeply felt defeats
we are convinced no one else can see.
Let me just say, in case it is helpful,

there isn't anyone here who doesn't understand
in personal ways—
at which you can only guess while we can only guess yours.

But I knew you when you were a child.
And I still see the same heart,
the same spirit alive amidst the hammering

of life. It is not a depressing thing
except that we might think it so.
It is a shared communion of suffering.

It is better than death, surely,
and better than thinking we are alone in pain.
It is your childlike spirit resisting the wearing-away.

It is your big heart,
your compassion, your soul.
Whispering against the fear.

It is all of the cosmic vibrations aligning you and me
and these words while I write them.
Maybe not whispering at all.

Maybe just saying it like it is:
Don't give up;
Embrace the blue and send it away.

Look it straight in the eye and remind it
we are the same purity who first opened our eyes
to this wild spectrum.

Give it a hug, and wave it
friendly,
out the door.

Familiar Storm

Outside there is, finally, snow.
Exactly what this fellow with a stormy soul wants.

The hardship of weather brings a police vehicle
and two employees running back to the door knocking,
young and vulnerable against the dark night.

There are batteries to start and there is scraping to be done.
I make sure their rear windshield defrost is on,
and the cabin is pumped full of heat.

My own car will start, I know it without a second thought.
And I will stay late to scrape, struggle, brush
against the ice.

I have done this before.
1996 and 1998 both had their dark, solitary, ice-ridden nights.
I am familiar with this.

Once they are all gone—
the employees, the police, the car which stopped by
to flirt or inquire—

I am left alone in the snowed parking lot
determining how slippery the roads will be.
And as I drive them, I push the peddle

hard now and then, just to slide a bit,
in order to know the conditions.
There are multitudes of flakes crashing

into my warm vehicle, Bob Dylan croons loud
against the feeble show of this weather.
It is only just starting to impress us.

There are no lanes visible.
For all the salt the endless circling trucks have thrown down,
everything is white.

It's very late to be driving.
I could put the transmission into second gear
instead of leaving it in automatic,

but there is fun to be had in seeing
how little this situation distresses me.
I do not want manual torque to prevent the spinning; I want the spin.

It's fun to hammer the throttle and
control the wheel—
watch the traction light blink as if I didn't already know.

It's all very selfish I suppose.
But there is no one around.
I am one with my spatial intelligence.

Then two things occur to me:
I smile when I am in a situation that requires serious thought;
There is something inside me which enjoys the metaphor of storm.

I am blessed by my curse and cursed by my blessing.
And so I watch the snow angle in from the blackness.
And I make a left turn, heading toward home,

thinking on snowflakes and poems.

Eliot's Epitaph

There is a book that has taken up residence on my nightstand.
It bears a note from my mother, in her handwriting
she can no longer make. A note from the past always present.

Better than a cellphone plugged in,
or my glasses resting until I use them,
this little book contains multitudes.

The most of which is the little note
my mother left to me,
never knowing if I would read it or even read

this little volume of TS Eliot.
"To Rob, my literate son who will appreciate T.S. Eliot's
Four Quartets," (underlined as she would do, my literate mother)

"as one poet enjoys the fine work of another."
She wrote it blue on an age-browned and fading page,
with binding glue dried out,

and a used bookstore sticker on the back.
She didn't worry about marking out the price—
as if to confirm what we both knew along:

Words are impermanent, but they are really all that matters.
The rest is paper and prices and noise.
The rest is the vacant into the vacant.

Call

I am called upon
from others
who are called upon

to give of ourselves
for them and each other.
Constant giving.

Constant always again
called upon,
love or dollars or help

advice among the mess,
work along the stretch
of a day.

It is not pretention.

We seek and call
like birds in nest
or falling through first-flight,

not knowing the difference.
Falling fast and calling
to each other.

My life has been catching.
To the point that I have fallen.
Giving the last broken bone in my wing

to the next bird who needs
a crutch for her wounds.
And I would do it again.

This is my call.

Disease

We carry these things
inherited
from our parents or siblings
slow walking stumbles with cane
stutters, shakes—
they've carried it before

and now it's our turn.
Pretending to be better;
that all is well.
Pretending that we won't pass
along the stutter or anxiety
to another generation.

God forbidding we pass
next generation disease.
Is the realization disease
or is the submission, we
wonder, slump, stutter, slam
into ancestral walls.

Sister talks little, except
when talking suits her.
Sister has anxiety—
ask her medication recommendations.
Sister found God,
she is closest.

Father told talk of learning
the value of a dollar.
Mother told talk of father
dying amidst papers
before his son died of
being an alcoholic asshole.

We tell talk tall tales
over papers on a desk
in the middle of the depression.
1939 here's a new prescription:
The truth is only the beginning.
Push to pull and then

do it again. Listen.
Pull. Tell talk ancestors
siblings parents children.
Quit when you don't want to.
Commit when you can't.
Learn to think about

how all of this is
stamped upon our lives
and yours and theirs
and even if you know best
your disease, well hell,
it knows better.

February

February is an odd month
with cold steeling the air.
It makes one wonder,
if the snow has caused a pause

or if we invited it?

Right now it's cold-crank frigid;
the battery doesn't really want to start.
There is a supernatural silence in the air
as if the molecules have gone somewhere to hibernate.

Even the windshield fluid is depleted:

a final fuck-you to the ridiculousness
of mercury being nowhere near the sun.
The weather folks say it's negative twenty
factoring in the windchill,

but at this point rhetoric is fanfare—

and we have no warmth for that.
Zero is cold enough,
or five, or put ten on top and it still
means nothing

when you're pushing down on jelly-peddle brake lines.

And as you drive,
the transmission moans strange sounds.
It's that kind of cold:
when everything says all of this would be better inside,

and all sane beings are resting.

February is so many layers of salt
on your car that you don't care anymore
how many layers are added.
February is a metaphor

reminding us there was a time

when we stood in the warmth
of another day past,

and sweated out droplets of purpose
and kinetic-energy drive.

Only to stand cold and silent

amidst the total bleak absence
of a house we used to know
or people we used to love
or times we used to enjoy.

Only to have everything frozen from us.

But that is far too depressing for the real point
about this month since I'm calling it out by name.
What I mean to say is, all of us were born
and have died—in one way or another—

in the cryogenics of February.

Growth in Winter

Baby is coming
in this cold winter with snow
teasing its way groundward through streetlights.

The darkness is cut
with white and a grouping of vehicles
spinning doughnuts in the parking lot like teenagers.

There is a part of me
cold and tired under coat,
that would rather be home and fed.

But this is what fathers do
without fanfare.

Somewhere in a warm womb
my child is dreaming of growing limbs
and heart-tempo songs.

It doesn't know
what awaits or even what awaiting means;
the outside snowing world does not exist.

And that is what mothers do
without fanfare.

Poem for a Wart

It's more than you deserve
and no doubt I will delete this after writing it,
just as you should be deleted.

You know that I've tried
six or ten times to burn you
out of existence.

But still you remain,
like a stubborn volcano
rising on the mantel of my pinky.

After each effort you get more Medusa on me—
to borrow from fables worth more than you.
You grow exponential from my efforts,

thicker and higher
as if trolling me with my own flesh,
while I think, "This time you're dead!"

I could take knife to you.
I could take saw or acid.
But you are the confident sneaky type:

you've woven yourself into me
and I can't manage the separation;
every effort makes you tougher.

I wonder, are you a metaphor
for my life?
Are you trying to tell me something

about resilience inherent in my own skin?
But now I'm writing to a wart.
That is certainly the last straw.

#Metoo Manhood

There are paths of cars intersecting each other
and metro trains
and people
in every mirror moving into each other

as if life were a Radiohead song.
They move like channels
or pre-ordained, spatial canals
the Venetians never could have predicted.

While he sits in his car,
feeling life race forward around him
without any participation—for fear.
There is no particular place where he belongs.

Even as he sits in his parked car
he is nervous it will be hit
by these steady moving vehicles.
And he will only hear tearing of metal and glass

and feel pain in his sudden-shock body.
All of these people in their capsules
are more valuable than he is,
even though they might share similar anxieties.

There is something that happens to a man
after a long time of being
significantly less,
or feeling somehow his sex

has marked him as wicked.
At first he grows determined to prove
he is good.
Then he endeavors to prove it to himself.

Next he relinquishes power
to abdicate whatever authority was presumed.
Then he loves everyone but himself.
And that's the tough part to surmount.

And he feels shy to speak in the masculine gender.
And he nods and complies.
And he sits in his car.

Wondering who put him here in the end,
with this keen observation of movement in the mirrors
and the realization he is not who he once was.

Clock

I wind my past,
tightening springs for time
in the future.

You are gone now;
but still the clock hangs,
waiting for revision of minutes.

As when I was a child,
key in hand,
I store kinetic self into this body of gears—

to be released in slow movement.
This clock and I, reach back
before memory's story.

Sad to see it neglected,
springs tired, not holding time.
But still I wind it.

I will take this clock,
its mechanisms cased in oak,
and fix it strong.

I will make it steady, level,
singing again, oiled, understood.
I will give it love to contain

its potential energy and release it.

Seven and Eight and Nine

It's been six years since I've seen you
except for every night
over and over again
like some kind of prophetic torture,
apologizing and professing my love.

In my dreams I stifle weeping.
I save you, or visit, or talk conversations.
I wonder at the marvel of your lives.
I've seen you grow.
In my mind's eye now you are eleven and nine.

I say, "Carly I'm so sorry, I love you and miss you
more than you can imagine."
I say, "Dylan I'm so sorry, I love you and miss you
more than you can imagine."
And there is peace in the torture.

I wake up,
realize the six years will continue to
seven and eight and nine.
And there is a clock moving gears
which used to rest on our mantel.

The world is dark and quiet.
I shift under the sheets to make myself warm.
But the catharsis is cheap;
nothing is ever resolved.
And I am the ancient mariner's wedding guest.

Or worse yet, and true, the captain—
albatross posing as my pillow,
while I sink back into the horrored glory of my dreams.

White Cat

White cat the city is not safe.
You are right, darting
your head left and right against the oncoming light
secretly tucked so no one sees you in total dark night.

The road between you and me
is not as dangerous as it seems but
I understand why you're hiding in your white self,
in the same way we've been brought together tonight.

Most hours I feel similar:
trying not to move and reveal myself
so that I too won't be accidentally run over
by people who don't see me along their hurry.

Maybe that's when I realize
both our furs are revealing,
and feel kindred with you.

As I watch without you knowing,
while you blend as best you can
on a bank of green ivy
near the sidewalk calculating ...

I want you to know I understand.
Just as, when it is safe for you
to move into the street which you
hadn't dared, you make a good effort:

Fast and determined at first,
then realizing the limits of pavement and cold
and the nauseating contention of awareness
and the realization that this space doesn't belong to you.

It's then I watch your ancestors
tell you not to run full speed into the middle,
but instead to be smart and stealthy—
to be the whole reason you're called "cat like."

I am with you in that ivy,
Hiding against the night
There are fears built into us,
But perhaps the pavement is a disguise

For things which can't restrain us.
Run and play.
Decide you own this street.
Tell anyone who argues with you to talk with me.

Locus Angst

Touch gently upon the subject you want to address.
Or do it loudly, but with regard.
And measure your voice.

I spent all day today and yesterday
running around accomplishing things,
noting other people's lack of intelligence and offensive body odor.

I felt guilty over these selfish observations—
which wouldn't have been as keen, if not
for the fact they were getting in the way of my productivity.

But really, in truth, I'm quite exhausted
with other people thinking they are never wrong.
We have a disease of external locus-of-control

in our society.
Though I suppose I'm arguing against my own point,
being disgruntled with the external.

I just don't believe in us very much anymore.
I think my youthful angst wasn't incorrect;
it was simply labeled by people who don't understand.

Red Shift

Life always wakes me up early and keeps me awake
even when I'm tired.

I can't remember sleeping in
like the other teenagers.

I read astronomy books in bed
and always got to school on time.

I lead physics classes
about the Doppler effect when the teacher was lazy
and passed the baton to me

as I broke track records
after a divorce

years before I had my own,
after having won of course

the first national prize for
my essay.

Now I am dealing with a shadow
on the door at 3:00 am
which is my own,

cast by a light across the street
I am negotiating with.

Is my shift blue or red?
I wonder which way my kinetic

interpretation of this angle of incidence
actually reflects my exhausted reality.

Where is the lens with which I can capture
this moment, and if I do,
will I be the only one awake?

Grow Legs and Walk

'Simple monkeys'
is the start of the easiest poem ever.
What say you?

Let's make it harder:

Skinny sex sells
in whatever language you speak
money is just a currency
put into the exchange
letting inhibitions
explode.

Simple.

Let's dig deeper:

Money is our agreement
of how we will
not
kill each other
even though we might want—
you can see where this hole
seeks to dig.

Now I'm presuming you kn
ow better.

Harder. Are you following?
on the page are
written words that can teach.

About trees and love and
birds. I know you are feeling dizzy fr
om the way language can be worked,
upon the visage of a husband and wife
talking across a dinner table.

Let's be honest:
of all the things I could have said
very surely this was not
ever the hardest.

The Eternal Space

I wonder what it is like
in your watery purse.

Are you dreaming, sleeping,
as you spin?

It must be all darkness
with perhaps a few muted red tones,

as if Picasso decided
to wash his brush upon your eyelids.

Then there is the sound of heartbeat,
and breathing and intestinal murmurs.

Sometimes, we are told, you can hear
our voices—

eager parents ready to meet you.
What is it like to grow in that dark space

inside liquid,
grasping the comfort of the cord winding out from you?

I was reflecting on this today,
as I thought about your arrival.

I realized without any particular fanfare,
that you don't really know the wonder of these concepts.

You don't know, or care that you don't know,
when or where you'll be born.

It doesn't concern you what year it is.
Or what country will be listed on your

certificate of birth.
I could be an astronaut or a prisoner, your father.

You don't know which is better or worse.
Or what any of it means.

Politics don't concern you in the least,

nor the root of the word 'politic' and how it came into being

in a language for which you have no preference or disdain.
Just as you aren't concerned

with generations of fathers
building this land or destroying it.

You bear no understanding of the implications of money.
Nor the concept of time, I think?

Perhaps I am wrong in that regard.
You are a mystery of complete Nirvana

and for that you outweigh me
in your one-pound brilliancy.

What permutations your existence might take.
What possibilities you hold.

You could be born to a tribe in Africa 10,000 years ago.
You could be born on a planet orbiting a star

inside Andromeda 10,000 years from now—
neither matters to you; these concepts hold no consequence of thought.

What a mystery, little one,
growing and playing inside the warm universe of your mother.

What a mystery,
from which all of us come.

I am grateful that you are in the eternal space.
Without anchors of thought.

The world will bring its weighty concepts upon you,
but for now—for the only time in your existence—

you are truly alive and free.

re-member childhood

long fences bounding sir
rounding

acres for a front
yard

a treasure map
crafted

aged
with *lipton tea* and buried

under mushroom damp
dug

that portal to an
other dimension be

cause eye
hadn't learned to

do it
on paper yet

deer
smashed near rail

road tracks
my childhood, walking

october new
england heir, atmosfear

trees
shaping in the night

knife
blade drawn-n-n-n

running
bloody Pequot lie

brary
hiding in books

muted snap
shot fading leaves

secret
ghosts in my eyes

Absence

How next level would it be
if I just left this poem empty
Like a plot of land after a tornado
Has ripped through?

All you'd read would be
snapped wheat grass and bent medal.
All you'd hear would be
sound of emptied atmosphere.

That would speak active-voice volumes.

Instead I am left staring
At the space beside me,
And wondering over the next line,
while talking to poets in my head.

I'm a sucker for fulfilment:
Nature abhorring a vacuum;
Osmosis drawing itself or being drawn into another:
Entropy creating a mess no matter how much we clean up.

This push and pull of absence appeals to me.

Perhaps there is something there,
If I look hard enough.
Perhaps the emptiness is actually full
of some misunderstood perspective.

There is one molecule in every three
square feet of the known universe
navigating gravitational pulls.
One little fellow finding his way

In a vastly larger absence.

Picture it: one molecule
smaller than a cell
and around it for millions of perspectives,
nothing but total and utter emptiness.

Everything you know, everything ever done,
Comes from that tiny existence in the middle
of complete vacancy.
It's almost overbearing-----too much.

And somehow all of that absence creates thunderstorms.

Black Dog

You shouldn't let your black dog run loose in the dark,
anyone knows that.
And there are leash laws, regardless of color or time.

The night is raindrop headlights
painting smears on mirrors, and your dog is standing in the street
sniffing puddles of nothing.

I only want to help, so after seeing him nearly hit by two cars
and a third one dutifully stopping
for what seems like an endless amount of time

not even honking the horn,
I reluctantly pull over to gather observational information.
Why is this dog seemingly abandoned at night?

I presume he is loved.
Maybe he has lost his home.
Perhaps someone is looking desperately for him

while we all dodge him with our cars.
Then there's a sign: he runs to a door.
It's the same door on the same brick home

smattering every block of this same city street—but he seems to know it.
I watch him claw intimately at the glass of the door.
A flashlight appears, scans from left to right and downward.

Thank goodness! He has found his owners!
But alas the door does not open.
He scurries again for the street, and I mutter aloud to no one,

"I really don't want to deal with this right now."
But of course I will because that's what needs to be done.
And either the dog needs help or the owners need to know

he is trying to come home, safely.
I had my own plans to do the same until he stood in the street;
I was going to write a poem about something else entirely.

Covid mask on, I slowly approach, and he barks.
I can read that his aggression comes from insecurity,
which is no surprise since I've secretly studied him these past few minutes.

He is small when he thinks no one is looking.
He is curious. He knows quite well he has little idea
how to navigate this world where no one has given him any answers.

The neighbor's dog starts to bark as he barks against me, looking tough.
It is entirely more noise than I intended to make, as a good Samaritan.
And the flashlight again appears through the door window,
scanning left to right, and down.

Goodness, open the door instead of fishing around
I think to myself.
And they do.

Two children appear, one brandishing the flashlight
swordlike into my eyes (I'll never know what she looked like).
The taller and presumably older one is a hefty black girl

to whom I explain the situation: "Two cars nearly hit your dog.
I was wondering if he or she is yours, and followed him or her
to your door."

I feel simultaneously proud and pissed that I am dealing with this
while also using proper grammar.
Most of me is simply trying to be done and go home.

But instead of resolution she asks, "What?" while her sister stabs me
in the eye with white, unspoken, insolence.
So I have to repeat the whole thing again

using altered words and expanding on the situation,
while still using proper grammar,
as I wonder why I chose to deal with this in first place.

"Okay," the black child says, and turns to the unseen adult
absent on a sofa somewhere while her children do the work
and her dog roams aimless in the late commute.

"He says Sammy almost got hit by a car."
And then closes the door.

Note to Myself

Freedom, the uncaging
of bird or body onto
bricks—freedom

You and I both know
the spaces between
the lines

We talk between then
and now, together
and honestly

I think your poems suck
as much as my own,
but sometimes

There is something there.
Something to cover
the mess.

You will be free, and sing.
I will save your words,
You will write them for me.

Muse

It's been too long since we have spoken.
I've been terribly snowbound, absent
but not for lack of trying.

Sometimes my schedule gets in the way
and life persists to annoy things,
and people are rude or kind.

Have I told you we are moving?
We're tacking down cotton
and sealing up the planks in the deck

to sail somewhere we have never been.
I apologize for the late notice;
it all happened rather quickly for me too.

We will be done with memory streets
and strangers we realize used to be friends,
and familiar frustrations we turn into poems.

I don't know how this will be, for us.
We've trekked from coast to coast,
and this is another leg in that journey

which may end soon or may not.
I might get hit by a truck, as they say,
or maybe we'll decide

it's all gotten too WAP for our tastes.
We have standards after all.
I just wanted to let you know I've been spinning

literal wheels among figurative ones.

And there was a moment today when I heard you
loud and clear, and when you heard me,
and I think that moment has always been with us.

It's a kind of shimmer on the surface—
like wind breathing over a lake.
You are the wind and I am the lake.

When you gather ozone to thunder,
I provide the water for rain.
A fact you already know, each night when you visit.

Do you sustain me or do I sustain you?
Is either answer mutually exclusive?
Schrödinger would be thoroughly bored.

But we trek on.
You call and I answer;
I call and you respond.

I am saying this to you now, my persistent muse:
we have something interminable.
This is our calling.

Without each of us, there would be absence.
I am not me without you.
And that's how I know

you think I've shared enough intimacy with our readers,
and should end with a resolving note.
As all good music does.

Circle Perspective

A bad card gets drawn—
as if life was luck of the draw.
Try as we might, this mystery

of breathing and loving and silence,
is not something we get along with very well.
And everyone always knows better than us.

And nobody trusts.
And everybody guesses.
And everything is all the crabs clawing us down.

This is not news to me;
that's the hardest part:
I have seen this all my life.

And nobody trusts.
And everybody guesses.
And everything is all the crabs clawing you down.

So let's get somewhere
since we're at the bottom,
in the circle of plastic that is life.

I think you think I think everything,
which is firing neurons
of circular logic and sadness seeing joy

just above the brim.
Every question of love is
just around the curve.

And we are always apart.
And we are always together.
And the madness of life is always.

How excellent it would be if we
could be alone with ourselves
and simultaneously understand each other.

Do our layers of experience
and sediment ego prohibit
that kind of connection?

I've seen this before.
Which is not to say I am immune.
This mess irritates me too, and I suppose I'm a part of it.

And I guess we are all alone.
And it's just as we were born.
And it's how we will die.

Rising above the brim,
remembering our love,
and the love of strangers

whom we didn't know
until we did.
And all the little monkeys think they know best.

And everyone seeks.
And everyone knows.
And all of this is us, being.

The Bird Feeder Outside My Window

There is a bird feeder
I placed outside my window
for cardinals or finches

For the first few days
the birds are still learning to know
it is there for them.

There is a metaphor in that.

My days have been work upon work
and loss and growth and hope
and survival under pressure.

I am learning this new home
like a bird finding a new tree
with a feeder hanging upon it

for the first time in its memory.

My wife and I are nesting
without gun shots and ambulances ----
we've upgraded

into a new life.
We're learning new memorizations
of where things are:

spices and pasta and silverware.

The world is one big restaurant,
all of us trying to navigate
Maslow's hierarchy of needs,

First comes the root of the tree
then the wood and branches, leaves,
and birds.

Still learning but grateful for the discovery.

Poet

You can do this for days and years.
Poet.
You can touch and tender the surface.

You have power for days and years.
Poet.
You can hear it and say it.

And when people read your words
they will know it.

There is no trick to the game.

There is only off-beat rhythm which you hear.

Counting off time while recording
the best and worst of everything.

You are internal rhymes missed but caught.
Poet.
You are circling sight.

You are recognition among the masses.
Poet.
You are circumstances understood.

Dark Figures

I wonder about the lives of all these dark figures,
and where they are going at night when I drive home.

It's too late for anyone to be heading toward a friend.
Too late, surely, to pick up groceries—

especially on foot.
But still they are walking.

Pandemic mask wrapped dutifully around their mouth and nose,
although there is no one else around.

Sweatshirt hoodie pulled over their heads
as if they are monks marking their progress with bells.

All of us should be at home, where our lovers or children sleep.
I am already sad for having closed the restaurant

where I work, only to make another
exhausted drive-by visitation with them.

Some wait at bus stops, hunkered and bored,
with a smart phone to distract their minds.

Others simply push onward,
foot by foot in the total blackness of night,

to reach whatever destination lies in the opposite direction.
Silent unseen martyrs of humanity.

I would like to stop and roll down my window,
ask their names and what holds them to this

tedious late-night journey.
But that would be awkward wouldn't it?

Better to simply pull over and wave these fellow travelers on board,
all of them, squeezing into my little sedan

as if it's a clown car.
I'll offer them all smiles and light their cigarettes.

Then one by one I'll drive them to their destinations.
While the whole time, along the way, we'll learn each other's stories.

Rain Clock Poetry

The antique clocks in my home
Compete with beats
to keep the minutes,
and I watch--- to see if the hands remain accurate.

They both keep good time, but there is always
the next minute.
The rain outside chimes
the keeping of another set of minutes

and I watch it from my cloud,

water drowning lights into puddles
streaking along thoughts
of moments
I can only try to translate,

while I pull my sweatshirt hood over
my headphones
and stand inside the rain
remembering childhood.

Not that any of it ever left me.

Dogwood trees and stacked-stone
walls. Scratching poetry about lichen
in the woods.
The reflection of rain on everything.

Teacher says I am a poet
when I am only ten
and I don't know what poet means.
Except I somehow do.

Nighttime with thoughts.

So I return to my clocks, steady in their place.
Making sense only to themselves
or perhaps only us,
but there is something here in this moment.

The rain and clocks have all gathered
these drops and moments,
determined to fall and click into the present with me
while I mark their perpetual progress.

Perhaps they are my muse
tapping me when a line
should be stopped
or a punctuation should

add itself or die.
Perhaps they are a reminder
of time and the erosion
of standing still trying

to make a poem.

Bong Hit

I'm an addict whose drug of choice is writing.
I've done it for 35 years

and when I don't hit the keyboard,
things get topsy turvy for me.

A mind tremor too subtle for you to notice
but too loud for me to ignore.

It's a slow drip of thought
keeping me on edge at day and

keeping me up at night.
It has me recite

over and over lines of poetry I've heard.
Tonight it was Dylan, who borrowed his name from the poet.

It's too hot to sleep, and time is running away.
For thirty minutes I played that line over in my head

trying to remember who sang it, and then realized
I'd named my first son after him.

When I don't write, I don't think well.
Happiness becomes slippery.

As I was exploring that thought tonight in the dark—
and considering larger ideas which come along

with such thinking about life's meanings
and where I should take mine—

it occurred to me I should type this confession.
That I should hit my keyboard

as if it is the tallest bong you've ever seen,
and you'd need a stool to reach your mouth on top of it,

and your friend would have to light the bowl
and your whole lungs would have to expand just in order

to get my words
inside you.

Movement

There are no stars here anymore,
no wonder in the sky
among the streetlights and sirens—
distraction and people calling,
saying move.

Move here, move with,
move blind, move distracted.
To me it seems like all shadows
and whispers saying,
"Move on."

I've been a part of this
noise for so long,
the only risk I run
is staying stuck in it.
Getting lazy inside inertia.

Not being able to see the stars
is only the smallest part,
when I sit outside and
recognize the air is something
I like but cannot enjoy.

This is not meant to be depressing;
this is something revelationary.
There is no point in looking
toward the sky when you
are trapped in a cage.

Perhaps there are no people
who care about the words
I am writing;
perhaps they think them simple.

Perhaps they think I'm only
a small man writing small things.
Perhaps they find no point
in looking toward the sky.

Perhaps they find no joy in thunder
or trees bending
against the wind, using
evolution to save their genetics.

The bend is not scary:
it is the exact purpose
of survival. Bend to grow;
grow, and you have to bend.

--

Our seed gets placed,
blown, moved, eaten,
processed by others,

before we have fibers,
we grow from dirt.
Our irony of birth is

necessary for our strength.
To see the sky we
must seek through dark.

--

There is a light
I can see

barely through the clouds.
I will touch it

--

and grow.

Barefoot Long Game

You saw a man today, walking barefoot, placing
each step along the tops of the parking space blocks—
or whatever those things are called that intend to tell a driver
he's driven the car too far forward.

He was walking a tight rope barefoot in the sun
while he held his smart phone a foot from his mouth,
talking speaker-phone to whoever was on the other end.

It made you think how far the world has come
since you were a boy, or—for that matter—a young man.

It made you think about age and time and how we still connect

to the beauty of a day, amidst all our devices and their
endless supernatural capabilities.

After all, he was walking a tight rope barefoot in the sun.
And he was gesticulating as if the person
on the other end of the conversation could see him.

You saw a man today, walking barefoot, placing
his words into the quick reality of a technological evolution
that cannot match the long game of our species.
And it made you smile.

Born Into Rain

There is mother bird outside my window
plucking worms from the earth—
two, three, five at a time—

and delivering them in her beak up to the dark, round, conical
nest in the tree opposite my door.
I watch her do it again and again, this loving commute.

Today has been a rainy day, which is why she's busy.
It occurs to me in my silly human fashion,
that the little baby birds must be getting wet!

And then it occurs to me:
birds are born in the rain.
It is no wonder they don't care when the sky

opens its moisture upon them.
They just fly on about their lives—
plucking out worms, or singing, or circling around a feeder.

It's the same with us, I think.
We are born in the rain.
All of life is born in the rain.

Pain which seems unfortunate to onlookers
is just ordinary to us.
We don't even register it.

It's like the parable David Foster Wallace quoted:
The two fish in the water and the one says,
"This is water," and the other responds,

"What's water?"
All of us are born into a wonderful, wet,
perfectly misperceived understanding

of existence.
This is what defines our lives—
our collective life on this planet.

Perhaps there are other planets where life
isn't born into rain,
where they don't understand the meaning
of shelter, or the lack of it.
We should not be jealous
any more than the birds are concerned for precipitation.

Those other creatures don't write about anything,
or create art, or struggle to understand
what they want to do next.

It is the tension that defines us.
It is the push and pull of adaptation that is the real gift
of our generational rebirth.

Whether we are the worm or the bird
the baby or the parent,
we are all alive in this way for the very fact

from the moment we are born
we share the same experience of our ancestors:
we are born into rain.

You are Here

You are here
struggling with the breath of life,
moving through each day,
dealing with the slander of existence.

You are here
waking up to birds or thunder,
deciding when to put your feet
on the ground beside your bed.

You are here
moving through the morning
into birdsong or bus smoke
or whatever beauty or pain awaits.

You are here
deciding that you are still alive
and choosing to navigate
the rest of the day which is the same

as your first or last.

Oxygen Deprived in a Cave with Plato

30,000 years ago we are
oxygen deprived
inside the cold recesses of a cave
watching shadows dance orange light
on the walls while we silently paint
handprints on the stone, getting high.

It is a membrane to another world.

We touch skin
dizzy cave firelight becoming educated
before you've written your allegory,
and create something
for the underworld and our minds
to play with.

See yourself there.

Cave dark fires and a pile of tinder
lit to illuminate
this communion
of smoke and echo sounds
and vision of the mind
while you put your hand against rock and blow ash

pigment to paint along our mother's face.

There is no reason for us to be
in the dark here together,
so far below the surface
where we can't see or breathe,
except that it is our nature
to pray to something.

Let me put my arm around your shoulder

and tell you of the things we will write,
while the twigs snap,
consumed by our fire.
You will write and men will speak
about your philosophy.
But for now, put your hand on stone.

Feel the grains of dirt beneath the tips of your fingers.

We will find ways to stamp
bricks and invent light,
print your words ten thousand times over.
For now, father, breathe the smoke
and relax into the creation of mother
pointing us toward the deep.

Become oxygen deprived.

Let go inside this space.
We will make strides after
this first step.
We will create the world together
for better or worse
while always ruminating thoughts.

For now, I'll take your hand and guide you

along the surface of our ancestors.
Oxygen deprived
seeking the light in the dark
of this cave with our shared fire
exchanging oxygen for illumination.
Now blow onto the surface of your hand

to answer questions we haven't yet asked.

Padding Around my Apartment Thinking on a King's Roux

I feel bad padding around
this small apartment
which doesn't contain nearly

half of what I can give.
I'd rather be a king,
walking on silk carpets

as the top of the
pecking order.
Then I wouldn't have to

listen to anyone
tell me without saying
I am really a disappointment.

I could pace around
and marvel at the artwork.
Admire this sculpture.

Smell that garden.
Flip a gesture to the chef
who'd deliver exactly the correct

dish with a gravy
built from the roux
of our deepest desires.

I wouldn't be arguing
with faucets that won't stop
dripping

or the neighbor smell
of marijuana.
I would just have the

faucet and the neighbor
duly executed
and move on to

playing chess in the sun.
Money wouldn't be a concern
of course

nor intimacy.
There'd be plenty of that.
I could finally

give you everything
you ever wanted.
And myself, for that matter.

I could turn this apartment
into a palace,
buy the entire building

and burn it down
for recreation.
Then establish

a royal decree
freeing all the animals
from butcher shops

and designating birds
as national treasures,
and placing bells

on the collars of every beloved cat.
Upon penalty of death
to the owners.

We could create our own
universe of exactly
how everything should be.

Exactly the right amount:
no more and no less.
We could determine

a four-day work week
and abolish registries
of all kinds

and place coal factories
on pink slip notices
and tell Elon Musk he must

stop stealing
our ambitions to put them
on Mars or into brain circuits.

We would forever ban
humanoid robots
because the inevitable result will be

sex slaves.
There would be a mandatory
walk each day

when we listened to nothing
except nature.
And we'd all grow

our own fruits and vegetables
after we first burned down
every single McDonald's.

Obviously we'd educate
every child at no cost
from the day they are born.

We'd abolish the GOP
and change its name
postmortem.

Pigs would become sacred,
and we'd parlay with them
to discuss strategy.

Bats would become
warriors,
and be respected as such.

And I'd pad around
our gilded palace
in the middle of the night

knowing nonsense
will be shot on sight
and tomorrow we will still

enjoy our kingdom.
Where everyone reads
and televisions are destroyed

and the revolution
has already won.
Where money is paper

scraps we use
to mulch trees,
returning the favor to them.

All clocks will become
analog and all measurements
will become metric.

People aren't allowed
to walk in a door
without checking behind themselves

to hold it open.
Or the door will close
upon their rude and now-concussed head.

People will learn to
think about the other
or they can shovel

their metaphors into
their own heads
in order to understand.

Together we will reform
child support completely.
While fathers don't see their children.

There won't be a need for
arguments over money
in which the loser is everyone.

It will no longer be the case
that a father's sperm is worthless
and the state can take 50%

of his slave income
while he tries to struggle out
of the hole he finds himself in.

The idea of poverty
as an elected state
that people want

will be summarily ridiculed
for the ridiculous idea it is.
And all of Fox News

and Q and
every other leach
sucking on the right wing

shall be removed and dropped
into the clouds beneath
the bird of our country,

to flail and die slowly
on the way down,
wondering how it got there.

With regrets to the families.
It had to be done
because they know not better

for the better good.
You'll understand
when you are able.

All of this will happen
because I've written it.
This is my padding

around the apartment thinking
upon the best damn
roux you've ever tasted.

There are poems that are worth
more than every statement
any person ever said.

There is something in art
that is so profound
other people who can't

duplicate it try to destroy.
It's the oldest story in history.
And history is just a poem.

Banging craniums against rock
and rock against craniums.
We already know we're better than this.

It must be the neanderthal
DNA within us
a relic of sex between two people

which still draws us to
beat each other down
when we know what is actually virtuous:

everyone should be able to eat
everyone should be able to learn
everyone should have shelter.

The premises of truth
are not punch lines
or arguments.

They are truth.
We know this.
And padding around they will

be instructed
not to think against
themselves or their brother.

There will be a place
where candles are lit
and nobody speaks.

I'll set it apart from the rest
of the messy world
so it is dark and noiseless.

We already know what
each other is thinking
with only a nod.

We need only eyes
to envision what the other
pair of eyes are thinking.

And there will be a button
I can push
to transform myself

into the child I was
at eleven
before you were even born

listening
to the pots clink
and trying to understand

why father
is upset with mother's gravy.
Or why she claims it so.

When I don't know
if her gravy was bad
or my dad was unfair.

Let's transmute
our flour and stock
into a roux

and get started.
While you've been reading
this I've been

snuggled in a tent
of certainty
that words are shadows

telling the truth.
So I will establish
a kingdom with roux

that always acknowledges
the right of the other person
to modify my kingdom.

Because I'm certain in his eye
there are experiences
I haven't had,

and I'll give him the chance
to explain them.
While also enforcing

equality for every
single
person.

Milton Keynes UK
Ingram Content Group UK Ltd.
UKHW030343240824
447344UK00001BA/154